All profits raised from the sale of this book will go to *Algerian Action*, a charity which assists poverty stricken children and families living in Algeria. To find out more please visit www.algerianaction.co.uk

A taste of Algeria

This book is meant to be just that, *a taste* of Algeria. The cuisine of this spectacular North African country is so vast and varied that it would take an entire library of books to really showcase the culinary delights and delicacies that the region has to offer. However, what this book attempts to do is to offer a glimpse into the Algerian kitchen, to provide a selection of delicious, authentic recipes both sweet and savoury for you to try at home.

All of the recipes found here have been generously submitted by women; home-cooks that have a connection with Algeria be it through birth, heritage or marriage.

Enormous thanks go to those ladies who contributed recipes and made the compilation of this book possible and of course thanks to you too dear reader, for buying the book and supporting the work of Algerian Action.

Happy cooking!

Emma Waller

(Charity founder)

Recipes

L'ham bi zitoun

L'ham lalou

Doubara

Tli tli

Lamb with artichoke

Tomatatish bil basal

Shorba Baida

Spiced fish tagine

L'kebab

Tajine kefta

Seafood and lamb sausage tagine

Karantita

Fish cakes

Dolma

Stuffed sardines

Berkoukez

Loubia

Lamb and green bean tajine

Mesfouf

Tajine zitoun

Kofte et pomme de terre au four

Chorba frik

Chorba Hamra

Rechta

Courgette salad

Carrot salad

Beetroot salad

Grilled pepper salad

Bourek

Cauliflower

Potato croquets

M'hadjeb

Lamona

Kesra

Beghrir express

Orange cake

Makrout with dates and honey

Basbousa

Mchakek

Mhalbi

Mhalbi #2

Griweche

Filled sables

Algerian shortbread

Kalb el louz

Halkouma

Mchewek

Makrout el louz

Nadia's cakes

H'rissa

Savoury recipes

Lham bi zitoun (lamb with olives)

This is a simple recipe that gives the juicy green olives centre stage. I have used lamb neck for this recipe, but it can be substituted with any cut on the bone. Don't forget to adjust the cooking time accordingly. This is a wonderful dish to serve in the centre of the table for guests!

Ingredients

(Serves 4)

1 tbs oil

1 onion, sliced

2 cloves garlic, finely chopped

½ tsp salt

1 ½ ras el hanout

½ kg lamb neck

2 tsp tomato puree

1l water

450g green olives, pitted

Method

Put a medium saucepan over a medium heat and pour in the oil. Add the onions and garlic and fry for five minutes. Stir in the salt and ras el hanout and cook for another two minutes. Brown the meat for five minutes then add the rest of the ingredients. Cover and cook for 45 minutes or until the meat is tender, topping up the liquid if necessary to ensure it just covers the meat and olives. Serve over chips or with bread.

Submitted by Amina Hachemi

L'ham lalou

A lamb dish sweetened with fruit.

(Serves 8)

Ingredients

2 1/2 lbs lamb, cubed

3 tablespoons butter

1/2 teaspoon ground cinnamon

3 cups water

50g sugar

16 prunes, soaked and drained (ready to eat)

2 tablespoons raisins

2 tablespoons almonds

1 pear, peeled and cubed

60ml orange juice

1 teaspoon orange blossom water (mazhar)

Method

Melt the butter in a big pan. Add the lamb and sauté for 5 minutes

Add the water, sugar and cinnamon. Mix well and cook over a medium heat for 40 minutes.

Add the prunes, raisins, pear and mazhar. Simmer for a further 15 minutes

Stir in the orange juice.

Take off the heat, mix well and serve.

Submitted by Umm Safia

Doubara

Serves 4

Ingredients

1 tbs. oil

4-5 garlic cloves finely chopped

2 tsp cumin

1 tsp paprika

½ tsp black pepper

1 tsp Salt

1 tbs tomato puree

¼ tsp harissa

4 tbs tinned chopped tomatoes or 2 large fresh

1 litre water

2 tins of chickpeas drained

3 tbs of finely chopped coriander

3 spring onions

Method

In a large pan add the oil, chopped garlic, cumin, paprika, black pepper, harissa and salt. Mix together and add the water and boil for 3 minutes.

Add the chickpeas, reduce to a medium heat, cover and cook for 15 minutes

Add the tomato puree and the parsley and cook for a further 25 minutes.

Serve hot garnished with chopped spring onions and a few leaves of coriander if desired.

Submitted by Emma Waller

Pasta with Chicken / tli tli

Ingredients

1 whole chicken chopped / 8 pieces of chicken on the bone

200g tinned chickpeas

2 tbs. butter or oil

¼ tsp black pepper

1 tsp tomato puree

½ - ¾ tsp cinnamon

2 minced garlic cloves

2 onions

Salt

3-4 eggs

1 chicken stock cube

500g orzo pasta

½ tsp Ras el hanout spice mix

Olive oil

Method

In a large pot add the butter/oil, finely chopped onions, ras el hanout, pepper, cinnamon and 240ml of water. Cook on a medium heat for 10 minutes.

Add the chickpeas, tomato puree and stock cube to the pot. Add more water, enough to just cover the content of the pot. Cover and cook on medium heat for 90 minutes.

Whilst this is cooking prepare the pasta and eggs.

Hard boil the eggs, peel and cut them into halves.

In a bowl, mix the pasta with 120ml water & a tiny bit of olive or sunflower oil. Place in a steamer & steam for 15 minutes. Remove from the steamer & separate the pasta with a little water.

Put the pasta in a large pan & slowly spoon in some sauce, a little at a time until the pasta is fully cooked & the sauce has been absorbed nicely - the pasta should be moist with a little sauce coating it - not dry.

Place the pasta in a large dish, top with the chicken pieces and add more sauce. Garnish with the egg halves.

Serve immediately.

Submitted by Umm Safia

L'ham bil khorchef (lamb with artichoke)

Ingredients

1 kg lamb

1 1/2 kg wild artichokes (khorchef)

1 onion, peeled and roughly chopped

3 garlic cloves, minced

1 tablespoon ghee (smen)

1/2 teaspoon ground cinnamon

100g chickpeas (tinned)

5 tablespoons chopped fresh parsley

2 lemons

1 tablespoon lemon juice

1 free range egg

2 pints water (approx)

salt and black pepper

Method

Prepare the Khorchef - wash thoroughly, remove stringy fibres and cut into pieces approximately 5cm in length. Place into a large pan of boiling water with 1 tbsp of lemon juice and boil for 10-15 minutes. Remove from pan and set aside.

Remove any fat from the meat and cut into 1" chunks. Chop the onion. Place the meat, onion and garlic in a large pan or casserole and fry gently on medium heat until meat is sealed and onion is lightly coloured.

Add the salt, pepper and cinnamon and cook for 10 minutes. Finally cover with water - approximately 2 pints, adds the chick peas and Khorchef.

Cover pan, bring to the boil before reducing heat and simmer for 1 hour. Check the seasoning and that the Khorchef is cooked (tender) and the chicken is well cooked.

Finely chop the parsley. Whisk the egg with the juice from 1 lemon and 4 tbsp of the sauce. Pour back into the pan mixing well and cook for a further 5 minutes on medium heat.

(Add a little stock if there is not enough sauce. Add a little water if sauce is too thick and is there is too much then cook for 5 minutes over high hid uncovered until sauce has reduced enough.).

 Serve this dish with a seasonal salad and fresh bread.

Submitted by Umm Safia

Tomatish Bil Bassal / Tomatoes with onions

So what to do when hubby brings home with an enormous amount of tomatoes, "because they were a good price" and *no* amount of salads will use up this glut of tomatoes?! Go Algerian and make *Tomatish Bil Bassal* or in English, Tomatoes with onions.

It is a tasty dish perfect for summer when tomatoes are cheap and all you need is some French baguette or other crusty bread on the side to mop it up with. Simply delicious!

Ingredients

4 large onions, halved and sliced

a few small chunks of meat, preferably on the bone to impart more flavour – however much you want to eat, I use 4 small chunks which is probably barely 100g

1kg chopped tomatoes

1 green chilli, deseeded (I recommend the use of rubber or latex gloves for this!)

salt

black pepper

1/4 tsp cinnamon

Method

Slice the onions and add them into a pressure cooker with a tablespoon of vegetable oil and a tablespoon of olive oil, add the meat and stir fry for a few minutes until the meat is sealed.

Roughly chop 1kg fresh tomatoes and deseed 1 fresh green chilli. I'd recommend using latex or rubber gloves when handling the cut chilli.

Throw the tomatoes and chilli into the pot with the onions and meat. Add a teaspoon of salt, 1/8 tsp black pepper and 1/4 tsp ground cinnamon, put the lid on the pot and leave to gently simmer for a while.

Liquid will start to come out of the tomatoes but after about 10 minutes add about a cupful or so of extra water and then screw on the pressure lid and leave on a low to medium heat for about an hour. Check the water level after about half an hour though.

Submitted by Umm Ibrahim

Shorba Baida

Ingredients

4 chicken legs

1 medium onion finely chopped

1 tin of chickpeas (approx 200g drained)

2.5 litres of Water

½ lemon –juiced

2 inch piece of cinnamon stick

3 tsp olive oil

Flat leaf parsley finely chopped

1 egg yolk

1 ½ tbs Basmati rice

Salt and pepper to taste

Method

In a large pot lightly fry the chopped onion in the olive oil. Add the chicken and cook for 8 minutes, turning the meat to seal it.

Add the water and salt and pepper. Cover and cook for 75 minutes on a medium heat.

Remove the chicken and debone. Place the chicken pieces back into the pot also adding the chickpeas. Cover and cook for a further 10 minutes.

Check the seasoning and adjust if required. Add the Basmati rice, again cover and cook for another 15 minutes.

Uncover; if the soup is too thick add a little more water at this stage if it is too thin cook uncovered until it reaches the right consistency.

In a small bowl whisk the egg yolk and lemon juice together. Add this to the pot stirring continuously as you do so. Cook for a further minute. Finally, take of the heat and add the parsley.

Serve with bread.

Submitted by Umm Safia

Spiced Fish Tagine

Ingredients

7 tablespoons olive oil

1/2 cup fresh coriander, chopped with heavy stems removed

4 garlic cloves

3 inches ginger-root, peeled and chopped

2 teaspoons ground cumin

1 teaspoon ground coriander

1/2 teaspoon anise seed

1/4 teaspoon cayenne pepper

salt, to taste

1 lemon, juice of

2 lbs fish steaks (firm white meat)

fresh ground black pepper, to taste

4 ripe plum tomatoes, halved lengthwise

1 medium onion, diced

1 red pepper, diced

1 green pepper, diced

2 cups eggplants, diced

1/4 cup pitted black olives

fresh coriander, chopped (garnish)

method

Place 4 tablespoons olive oil in blender with coriander, garlic, ginger, cumin, anise, cayenne pepper, 1/4 teaspoon salt and lemon juice. Process until smooth.

Cut fish in 4 or 6 portions. Season with salt and pepper. Place in dish, and coat with mixture. Marinate 2 hours.

Meanwhile, heat oven to 300°F. Place tomato halves in tagine or in baking dish. Brush with 1 tablespoon olive oil, season with salt, and bake 1 1/2 hours, then chop coarsely.

Heat remaining oil in skillet. Add onions and peppers, and sauté about 5 minutes. Add eggplant and sauté 5 minutes longer. Add tomatoes and olives. Season to taste.

Place mixture in tagine or in baking dish, or leave in skillet if it is ovenproof and has a cover. Place fish on top of vegetables. Cover tagine, baking dish or skillet. Place in oven to bake for 20 to 30 minutes, or simmer on top of stove over low heat, about 15 minutes. Garnish with coriander and serve.

Submitted by Riana Nel

L'Kebab

Not the grilled meat, salad and pitta bread that one might imagine. Instead this is a dish made up of chicken and chips with egg thrown in- really, it tastes much nicer than it sounds!

Ingredients

500g chicken pieces

1 large onion finely chopped

1kg potatoes

4tbs oil

Handful chickpeas

5 tbs flat leaf parsley finely chopped

2 eggs

1 lemon (juice of)

½ tsp cinnamon

1 tsp Salt

½ litre Water

Method

In a large pot place the oil, chicken pieces, salt and cinnamon and cook over a low heat for approximately 8 minutes until the meat is sealed and the onions softened.

Add the water and chickpeas to the pot cover and continue to cook.

Peel the potatoes and cut them into chips. Heat the oil and fry the chips until they are almost cooked but not golden in colour. Set aside.

Take 5 tablespoons of the water (which should be becoming sauce like) from the pot and put it into a small bowl. To this add the lemon juice, the eggs and flat leaf parsley. Lightly whisk together and then add it to the pot.

Add the chips to the pot. Cover and cook for a further 8 -10 minutes.

Serve hot garnished with a few parsley leaves if desired and crusty bread.

Submitted by Emma Waller

Tajine Kefta

This is a tasty winter dish that is basically, an Algerian version of meatballs in sauce.

Ingredients

<u>For the sauce</u>

1 large onion finely chopped

6 large fresh tomatoes / ¾ tin of tomatoes

1 tbs paprika

1 tsp cumin

½ tsp Cayenne pepper

3-4 tbs flat leaf parsley finely chopped

2 cloves of garlic finely chopped

½ tsp salt

½ tsp black pepper

1 tbs vegetable oil

water

<u>For the meat</u>

1 tbs paprika

1 tsp cumin

½ tsp cayenne pepper

3 tbs flat leaf parsley

2 garlic cloves

½ tsp salt

¼ tsp black pepper

500g minced lamb or beef

Method

In a large pan add all of the ingredients for the sauce except the water. Simmer over a low heat for approximately 10 minutes so that the onion softens and the flavours begin to meld together.

Whilst the sauce is cooking prepare the meat by mixing all of the ingredients in a bowl together. Divide and shape into walnut sized balls.

Check the sauce; if it is beginning to dry out a little add 2 tbs water so that it doesn't burn. Now place the meat balls into the pot leave for a few minutes until the meat has sealed and taken on a little colour.

Add the water, cover and simmer for a further 20 minutes.

Garnish with additional parsley leaves and serve alone with bread or accompanied with couscous.

Submitted by Emma Waller

Seafood & Lamb Sausage Tagine

Ingredients

500g white fish fillets cut into 4cm pieces

400g cleaned baby octopus, halved lengthways

12 (about 400g) large green king prawns, peeled leaving tails intact, deveined

1 red onion, halved, thinly sliced

2 baby fennel bulbs, trimmed, quartered lengthways, fronds reserved

2 large celery sticks, trimmed, thickly sliced diagonally

2 tbs olive oil

2 tsp sweet paprika

1 tsp ground cumin

1 tsp caraway seeds

1/2 tsp dried chilli flakes

125ml water

6 (about 450g) lamb, mint & rosemary sausages (Lamb Merguez)

Method

Combine the fish, octopus, prawns, onion, fennel, celery, oil, paprika, cumin, caraway seeds and chilli flakes in a bowl. Transfer to a 3L (12-cup) capacity flameproof tagine. Add the water. Cover and cook over low heat for 40 minutes or until the seafood is cooked through. Set aside for 10 minutes to rest.

While the tagine is resting, preheat a char grill on medium. Cook the sausages, turning, for 8 minutes or until cooked through. Thickly slice diagonally.

Top the tagine with the sausage and reserved fennel fronds.

Submitted by Riana Nel

Karantita

This is a typical Algerian 'street food' which is very easy to prepare.

Ingredients

240g chick pea flour (gram flour)

950ml of water

120ml vegetable oil

1 tbs salt

¼ tsp black pepper

1 egg

½ tsp Ground cumin

Method

Put the flour, vegetable oil, water, salt and pepper into a large bowl and whisk together, either by hand or with an electric blender.

Pour the mixture into a greased dish.

Whisk the egg and pour over. Sprinkle with the cumin and bake in the oven at 375f for approximately 1 hour. The Karantita is ready when it is firm but still a bit wobbly.

This is usually enjoyed sliced and sandwiched in crusty bread with a generous serving of harissa/ hot pepper sauce.

Submitted by Umm Amina

Fish Cakes
Ingredients

175g (6oz) chopped onion

Salt

100g (4oz) breadcrumbs

150mls (1/4 pint) milk

3 eggs

675 (1 1/2 lbs) fresh white fish such as haddock, cod, whiting etc

Black pepper

1/4 teaspoon ground cinnamon

1/4 teaspoon ground cloves

Flour for dusting

Butter and olive oil for frying

Method

Sprinkle the onions with salt and leave aside for half an hour

Soak the breadcrumbs in the milk for about 10 minutes then squeeze them until most of the milk has gone

Beat the eggs and add this to the breadcrumb mixture

Chop the fish and the onions very finely; you can use your food processor here for convenience.

Season with the cinnamon, cloves and black pepper.

Leave the mixture in the refrigerator for half an hour.

Finally, form the mixture into round cakes and dust with flour.

Fry them gently in the butter and oil until golden brown

Serve with a fresh green salad.

Submitted by Riana Nel

Dolma

This recipe makes a tasty dish made up of mince stuffed vegetables and a red sauce.

Ingredients

For the meat

1 lb minced lamb

1 large onion finely chopped

1 tbs tomato puree

½ tsp black pepper

½ tsp salt

Few drops of harrisa or hot pepper sauce

2 garlic cloves finely chopped

3 tbs flat leaf parsley

3 tbs coriander

1 tbs olive oil

6 tbs fresh bread crumbs

2 large courgettes

6 medium potatoes

For the sauce

1 tbs vegetable oil

2 garlic cloves finely chopped

1 tsp ras el hanout

½ tsp paprika

½ tsp salt

¼ tsp black pepper

Method

Place all of the sauce ingredients into a large pot, stir together and set aside.

In a bowl mix all of the 'meat' ingredients together except your vegetable selection. Mix together and set aside.

Wash your vegetables and peel the potatoes. I personally like to use courgettes and potatoes but other types of vegetables can also be used. Cut the courgettes into 1" chunks and cut the potatoes in half. Hollow out the middles of the sliced vegetables and stuff with the mince mixture. Place these into the pan. Any remaining mince can be formed into walnut sized meatballs and added to the pot.

Cook everything for a few minutes over a medium heat to seal the meat and soften the onions slightly. Add enough water to just cover the contents of the pot, cover and allow to simmer until the water has been reduced to a sauce (approximately 40 minutes).

Serve hot with fresh bread.

Submitted by Emma Waller

Stuffed Sardines

Sardines are a popular fish in Algeria and the shouts of sellers of this fish can be heard regularly in the morning. The first time I tasted this dish, it was made by Kamela, a very dear friend of my in-laws and now, of mine too. It makes a perfect lunch when served with salad and fresh crusty bread.

Ingredients

1kg of fresh sardines

6 tbs finely chopped flat leaf parsley

3 cloves of garlic finely chopped

1 lemon-juiced

½ tsp salt

1 tsp cumin

1 tsp paprika

Flour

Oil for frying

Lemon wedges (optional)

Method

De-head, wash and remove the backbones of the sardines. Set aside.

In a small bowl mix together the flat leaf parsley, lemon juice, salt, cumin and paprika.

Lightly fill each sardine with some of the parsley mixture and dust the outside with flour. Once all of the sardines have been prepared in this way fry them in hot oil until golden. Drain on tissue.

Serve hot garnished with a few parsley leaves and lemon wedges.

Submitted by Emma Waller

Berkoukez.

Vegetables and pasta pellets served in a delicious sauce.

Ingredients

1 Potato Diced,

1 Carrot Diced

1 Courgette Diced,

1 Onion Diced,

1 tsp Garlic,

1 tsp Paprika,

1 tsp Ras el Hanout,

1 tbsp Tomato Paste,

Salt & Pepper,

A vegetable stock cube,

water,

Berkoukez.

Method

Cook the potato, carrot, courgette, onion and garlic in oil to soften for 5-10 minutes.

Add the paprika, ras el hanout, tomato paste, salt and pepper and a stock cube and slowly start to add water.

Keep adding water every so often and towards the end add 1 coffee-mug full of Berkoukez. Cook for another 20-30 minutes until the Berkoukez is swollen and cooked. Be careful at this stage because the Berkoukez soaks up a lot of the sauce so more water may be needed.

Submitted by Umm Youcef

Loubia

Algeria's version of baked beans- only a touch more sophisticated!

This dish can be made very quickly and optionally can include meat.

Ingredients

1tbs vegetable oil

3 cloves of garlic –finely chopped

I large onion finely chopped

Itsp salt

¼ tsp paprika

½ tsp black pepper

1 bay leaf

4tsp cumin

1 tsp tomato puree

2 large fresh tomatoes

500g tinned haricot beans (or the equivalent in pre-soaked, ready to use dried beans)

100g cubed lamb /beef (optional)

Method

Add the oil, garlic and onion (and meat if using) to a pot. Cook over a medium heat until the onions soften and the meat is sealed.

Add 1 cup of water to the pot

Add the salt, black pepper, cumin, paprika and bay leaf to the pot. Stir.

Add the tomato puree and tomatoes to the pot. Cover and simmer for 5 minutes.

Add the haricot beans and a further three cups of water to the pot. Cover and simmer for approximately 20 minutes until the water reduces down to a sauce/ soup like consistency.

Check salt and pepper to taste, add a dash more cumin if desired.

 Serve hot, drizzled with olive oil and accompanied with fresh crusty bread.

Submitted by Emma Waller

Lamb and green bean tajine

(Serves 4)

Ingredients

1 tablespoon oil

300g Cubed lamb

2 medium onions (1 finely chopped, 1 sliced into rings)

4 garlic cloves finely chopped

1 tsp salt

¼ tsp black pepper

½ tsp cayenne

2 tsp cumin

½ tsp turmeric

2 tomatoes roughly chopped

4 tbs chopped fresh flat leaf parsley

1 ½ lb green string beans trimmed

Method

Put the vegetable oil, garlic and onion into a large pot. Cook over a medium heat until the onions are softened and the meat sealed.

Add the salt, pepper, cayenne, turmeric and 1 tsp cumin to the pot. Stir.

Add water, tomatoes and green beans. Cover and simmer for 40 minutes.

Add the sliced onion rings, parsley and 1 tsp cumin. Simmer for an additional 10 minutes.

Serve hot either as is with fresh bread or poured over couscous.

Submitted by Umm Hashim

Mesfouf

This is a popular dish consisting of couscous, peas and broad beans.

Ingredients

250g peas

250g broad beans

300g couscous

Salt and pepper to taste

1tsp olive oil

1 tbs butter

Olive oil for drizzling

Method

In a bowl place the couscous and a little water to just moisten it, mix through.

Add the olive oil and again mix through thoroughly to ensure that there are no lumps and the oil is evenly distributed.

Tip the couscous into a steamer, cover and steam for approximately 10 minutes.

While this is steaming start to prepare the vegetables by boiling them until cooked, drain and set aside. Alternatively steam the vegetables until cooked and set aside.

Remove the lid from the couscous, sprinkle with water and lightly mix through. Cover and steam for a further 5 minutes.

Add the cooked vegetables to the steamer, cover and steam for 3 minutes.

Tip the contents of the steamer into a large bowl, add a tablespoon of butter if using and salt and pepper to taste. Mix through thoroughly drizzle with olive oil and serve hot.

Traditionally this dish is eaten accompanied with a big glass of buttermilk

Submitted by Umm Nabil

Tajine Zitoun (chicken and olive tajine)

This is a really delicious way of serving chicken. The olive stew flavoured with lemon and coriander offers a nice light sauce making the dish suitable for eating during the warmer months as well as in the winter.

Ingredients

1 tbs vegetable oil

1 whole chicken, skinned and chopped into 8- 10 pieces

1 medium onion finely chopped

½ tsp salt

¼ tsp black pepper

1/4 tsp ground ginger

½ tsp cinnamon

½ tin of plum tomatoes or 2 fresh tomatoes

6 garlic cloves finely chopped

3 large carrots- peeled and sliced into thin rounds

6 tbs fresh flat leaf parsley finely chopped

6 tbs fresh coriander finely chopped

Peel of 1 lemon

300g Green olives (pitted)

Water

Method

In a large pot place the onion, vegetable oil and chicken.

Cook over a medium heat until the onions are softened and the meat sealed.

Add 3 tablespoons of water to the pot in addition to the garlic, salt and black pepper. Stir.

Add the cinnamon, ginger, flat leaf parsley and coriander.

Add the tomatoes and sliced carrots.

Add 500ml of water and bring to the boil.

Reduce the heat cover and simmer until the chicken is cooked through.

Remove the chicken and half the carrots from the pot and set aside.

Add the olives and lemon peel to the pot and increase the heat slightly. Cover and cook for three minutes. The sauce should now be thickened if it is still too watery continue cooking until it is the desired consistency.

Return the chicken and carrots to the pot, stir through.

Garnish with a few coriander leaves.

Serve hot.

Submitted by Emma Waller

Köfte et pomme de terre au four

A simple yet delicious oven baked dish made from potatoes and minced meat.

Ingredients
500g ground meat
3 large potatoes, peeled and sliced
2 onion, finely diced
2 tsp cumin
1 tsp cinnamon

1 tsp coriander, ground
3 garlic cloves, finely minced
1 TBS butter
3 TBS tomato puree
Juice of half lemon
1/2 cup water
1 TBS olive oil
Handful of roughly chopped parsley
salt/black pepper

Method

In a large bowl, add the meat, butter, 1 onion, salt, pepper, cumin, cinnamon, parsley and garlic, mix well.

Shape meat into balls. Set aside.

In a pan, sauté the other onion in the olive oil until golden.

Add in the remaining ingredients and simmer for 15 m until a thin sauce forms.

Now butter or oil a baking dish, then arrange the meatballs and potatoes in the bottom.

Pour the sauce over the meat and potatoes.

Bake in the oven at 180 deg for about 30 minutes until the sauce has thickened.

Serve with lots of bread to mop the sauce.

Submitted by Henrietta Takács El-Ghoul

Chorba Frik

A delicious soup that is slightly spicy. It can be eaten all year round but is a favourite during the month of Ramadan.

Ingredients

(Serves 6)

1 tin (400g) of plum tomatoes

1 tin (200g drained) of chickpeas

1 large onion finely chopped

1 medium courgette, trimmed and halved lengthways

2 sprigs of fresh mint

6 tbs coriander finely chopped

1.5 litres water

1 tsp tomato puree

½ tsp black pepper

½ tsp paprika

¼ tsp cinnamon

¾ heaped tbs ras el hanout

1 tbs salt

300g Lamb cut into small chunks

2 tbs frik (bulgar wheat)

Method

Put the frik (bulgar wheat) into a bowl and add enough warm water to just cover the contents. Set aside.

In a large pot add the meat, onion, salt and pepper. Cook over a medium heat until the onion softens and the meat is sealed.

Add a few tablespoons of water to the pot to prevent the onion burning. Add the cinnamon, paprika and ras el hanout and stir.

Add the 1.5 litres of water, the chickpeas, plum tomatoes, courgette, coriander and mint to the pot. Reduce the heat to low, cover and allow to cook for 45 minutes.

Remove the mint sprigs, courgette and tomatoes from the pot and blend together to form a pulp. Return this to the pot and stir through.

Drain the frik (bulgar wheat) and add it to the pot. Allow to simmer for a further 2 minutes.

Serve hot accompanied with fresh bread and bourek.

Submitted by Emma Waller

Chorba Hamra

Exactly the same as Chorba Frik but instead of adding Frik (bulgar wheat) vermicelli is used.

Ingredients

(serves 6)

1 tin of plum tomatoes

1 tin of chickpeas

1 large onion finely chopped

1 medium courgette, trimmed and halved lengthways

2 sprigs of fresh mint

6 tbs coriander finely chopped

1.5 litres water

1 tsp tomato puree

½ tsp black pepper

½ tsp paprika

¼ tsp cinnamon

¾ heaped tbs ras el hanout

1 tbs salt

150g Lamb cut into small chunks

2 handfuls of dried vermicelli

Method

In a large pot add the meat, onion, salt and pepper. Cook over a medium heat until the onion softens and the meat is sealed.

Add a few tablespoons of water to the pot to prevent the onion burning. Add the cinnamon, paprika and ras el hanout and stir.

Add the 1.5 litres of water, the chickpeas, plum tomatoes, courgette, coriander and mint to the pot. Reduce the heat to low, cover and cook for 45 minutes.

Remove the mint sprigs, courgette and tomatoes from the pot and blend together to form a pulp. Return this to the pot and stir through.

Crush the vermicelli and sprinkle it into the pot. Allow to simmer for a further 4 minutes.

Serve hot accompanied with fresh bread and bourek.

Submitted by Emma Waller

Rechta

Algerian noodles with chicken and a light sauce.

Ingredients

(Serves 8)

<u>For the Rechta (noodles)</u>

500 g plain flour

1/2 teaspoon salt

Water

cornflour, to aid rolling out

1 tablespoon ghee (smen)

For the sauce

1 1/2 kg chicken pieces

2 onions finely chopped

1 garlic clove, minced

1 tablespoon sunflower oil or 1 tablespoon vegetable oil

200g of tinned chickpeas

1/4 teaspoon black pepper

2 1/4 teaspoons ras el hanout spice mix

1 litre water

1 teaspoon cinnamon

500 g long turnips cut into 6ths

250 g potatoes, quartered

250 g courgettes cut into 6ths

1½tsp.salt

For the Rechta noodles

Sift the flour into a large bowl. Add the salt and make a well in the centre. Add a little water and mix to form a firm but slightly soft dough.

Divide the dough into quarters and roll each quarter out to an approximately thickness of 1-2mm on a surface dusted lightly with cornflour.

Dust the dough sheets very lightly and put through the pasta machine on the lowest setting (to create thinnest pasta sheet). Once all of the pieces have been put through the machine, put them on the side to dry out a little - for approximately 20-30 minutes.

Change the setting or add the attachment on the pasta machine to the one that cuts fine ribbons. Pass the sheets through the machine. Dust each sheet with cornflour- this really helps the noodles not to stick together.

Allow to rest for 10 minutes before steaming. Take a tiny amount of oil on your hands and gently rub a little through the noodles to prevent them from sticking together whilst cooking.

Once the steam rises from the noodles, cook for 5 minutes. Remove from the couscousier /steamer and sprinkle a little water over it and separate any noodles.

Return to steaming for a further 5 minutes or until noodles are visibly cooked.

Tip the noodles into a large dish and gently mix the ghee (smen) through it. Taste and add extra salt if required. Set aside.

For the sauce

In a pressure cooker, fry the onion, garlic and chicken in the oil with the spices, cook for further 10 minutes on medium heat.

Add the vegetables and chick peas and pour on the water. Season and cook for 30 minutes or until chicken and vegetables are tender.

*If you do not use a pressure cooker, cook for approximately 1hr and add the chickpeas during the last 20 minutes of cooking time.

Serve the rechta by placing the rechta noodles in a large dish then pour approximately half of the sauce over the top. Arrange the vegetables and chicken on top so that they are evenly distributed

Traditionally rechta only has turnip in it. My family prefers the above mix of vegetables and sometimes I even add carrots - you can use what you like!

Submitted by Umm Safia

SIDE DISHES

Courgette Salad

Ingredients

500g Courgettes

¼ tsp black pepper

½ tsp salt

¼ tsp cumin

½ tsp vinegar

1 tbs olive oil

3 garlic cloves

1 tbs. chopped flat leaf parsley

Method

Wash and thinly slice the courgette into rounds.

Place the prepared courgette into a pan of water and add the salt, black pepper, cumin and bay leaf. Boil for approximately 18 minutes until the courgettes are cooked but still retain their shape.

Drain well and place onto a serving plate.

In a small bowl mix the olive oil, garlic and vinegar together to make a dressing. Pour this over the courgette and finally, sprinkle over the chopped parsley.

This can be eaten hot or cold.

Submitted by Emma Waller

Carrot salad

Ingredients

500g carrots

3 cloves of garlic

1 lemon juiced

2 tbs. Olive oil

½ tsp salt

3 tbs chopped flat leaf parsley

½ tsp black pepper.

Method

Wash and chop the carrots into small cubes.

Place and boil in a pan until cooked.

Drain thoroughly.

In a small dish mix the garlic, salt, pepper, olive oil and lemon juice together to make a dressing.

Toss the carrots in the dressing and then mix in the parsley.

Cover and place in the fridge for at least an hour for the flavours to meld together.

This can be eaten alone but, I prefer it sprinkled through a green salad or something similar.

Submitted by Umm Imran

Beetroot Salad

Ingredients

500g Beetroot

2 tomatoes

I small onion-grated

2 tbs finely chopped flat leaf parsley.

2 tbs. olive oil

1 tsp vinegar

½ tsp salt

Method

Wash and trim the beetroot and boil in a pan of water until cooked (this step can be skipped by using beetroot that has already been cooked)

Cut the beetroot into thin slices add the grated onion.

Chop the tomatoes into similar sized slices and set aside.

In a separate bowl mix the oil, vinegar and salt to make a light dressing, pour this over both the beetroot and tomatoes.

On a serving plate arrange the tomatoes and beetroot and garnish with the parsley.

Submitted by Nabila Demsiri

Pepper Salad / H'miss

A delicious salad that tastes great with grilled meats or just simply scooped up with fresh crusty bread.

Ingredients

Serves 4

4 red peppers

2 tomatoes

2 tablespoons of olive oil

Salt to taste

Method

Wash the peppers and tomatoes and place them on the grill. The aim is to completely blacken the skins. Once this is done place them into a plastic bag or wrap in cling-film. Leave for 5 minutes.

Take the tomatoes and peppers out of the plastic and rub the blackened skins off. Do not wash them otherwise the flavour will be lost.

Deseed the peppers and cut into long thin strips. Place these strips and the tomatoes in a bowl and lightly mash them together. Add salt to taste and drizzle with the oil.

Submitted by Umm Hashim

Bourek

Bourek is a much loved appetiser throughout the whole of Algeria.

They are made from a very fine pastry known as dioul or in French feuille de brik, these can be purchased in the UK from North African butchers / grocers but as an alternative spring roll sheets can be used.

The pastry can be filled with almost anything. Popular choices include minced lamb, tuna, cheese or chicken which are mixed with mashed potatoes, olives, onions…………really the options are endless.

Bourek filled with lamb and olives

Ingredients

10 dioul sheets

120g Minced lamb

1 small onion finely chopped

1 tbs finely chopped flat leaf parsley

½ tsp salt

¼ tsp black pepper

3 large potatoes peeled and quartered

20 green pitted olives, finely chopped.

4 cheese triangles or similar.

Oil for frying

Lemon wedges to serve

(makes 10)

Method

Boil the potatoes until cooked through. Mash and set aside.

While the potatoes are boiling prepare the lamb by placing it in a frying pan with the onion, salt, pepper and parsley. Cook until just done, do not let the meat become too dry.

Once both the mashed potato and lamb is prepared and had a little time to cool you are ready to assemble the bourek.

Take one dioul sheet and lay it flat. Approximately 5cm up from the bottom Of the sheet place 3 tablespoons of mashed potato, one next to each other lengthways. Next take two tablespoons of mince and sprinkle this over the mashed potato. Take a teaspoon full of the chopped olives and sprinkle this over the mince. Take two small chunks of the cheese and add these to the filling.

Now bring up the bottom of the sheet so that it comes up to/ covers the filling and roll over once. Take each side of the pastry and fold it in towards the centre of the sheet. Continue rolling the bourek up until the end of the sheet. Do this for all of the dioul sheets.

In a large frying pan heat the oil, enough to shallow fry the boureks. Once the oil is hot place the boureks into the pan, ensuring the closure is at the bottom. Fry for a few minutes and then turn to cook the other side. The boureks should be golden brown in colour.

Remove from the pan and drain on kitchen paper.

Serve hot with lemon wedges on the side.

Submitted by Emma Waller

Cauliflower

This is a nice flavoursome way to serve cauliflower. It is particularly nice with roast chicken.

Ingredients

1 cauliflower head chopped into pieces

Water

1 tsp salt

1 tsp cumin

½ tsp black pepper

2 tablespoons oil

3 garlic cloves finely chopped

Method

Boil the cauliflower until it is halfway cooked, drain and set aside.

In a pot place the oil, garlic, salt, pepper, and cumin. Add the partly cooked cauliflower and toss in the oil/spice mixture. Add enough water to just cover the cauliflower. Cover and cook over a medium heat for approximately 15 minutes, the water should be significantly reduced, if there is still a lot remaining continue to cook for a further few minutes. Tip out into a bowl and sprinkle with a little more cumin to serve.

Best eaten hot.

Submitted by Nabila Demsiri

Potato croquets

Ingredients

A delicious finger-food made up of a soft potato and cheese filling and a crispy outer coating.

6 Potatoes, peeled and quartered

1 onion finely chopped

1 tsp salt

½ tsp black pepper

2 tbs flat leaf parsley, finely chopped

6 Cheese triangles or other soft cheese.

2 eggs, beaten

Flour, seasoned with salt and pepper

Oil to shallow fry

Method

Boil the potatoes until soft, mash and set aside to cool.

Mix the mashed potatoes, onion, salt, pepper and parsley together.

Form the mixture into golf ball sized spheres.

Taking each ball in turn, push a small blob of cheese into the centre and close up. Press down slightly to form a patty shape.

Dip the patties into the egg and then the seasoned flour.

Heat the oil and once hot fry the patties for a few minutes each side, they should be golden brown in colour.

Drain using kitchen paper.

Serve hot.

Submitted by Emma Waller

M'hadjeb

An Algerian speciality that is made up of a semolina based dough filled with tomatoes and onions. The recipe is written below but really it is so much easier if you can watch a person make it first.

Ingredients

For the dough

1 kg semolina

1 tsp salt

Water

For the filling

3 fresh tomatoes

2 Onions

Salt

Pepper

Oil

Method

To make the dough- put the semolina and salt into a large bowl. Gradually add water until the semolina comes together to form a dough. Turn the dough out onto a work surface and begin kneading. To prevent the dough from drying out keep sprinkling it with water.

Continue kneading and sprinkling with water for approximately 30 minutes. The aim is to create a soft, manageable dough that when pulled becomes almost transparent.

Cover and set aside for 30 minutes while you prepare the filling.

To make the filling- finely slice the onions and put in a pan with the salt, pepper and oil, sauté until soft. Add the tomatoes and stir through. Simmer until the mixture thickens.

Return to your dough; divide into balls about the same size as a small orange. Taking one at a time begin rolling and pulling out the dough into a large square-ish shape. Use a little oil to manipulate the dough and to avoid it sticking to the work surface. This does take some practice but, the dough should be pulled so thin it's almost like gauze.

Once this is done spoon two or three tablespoons of filling into the centre, it should be spread quite thinly to avoid it splitting the dough.

Now pull up and fold over the bottom of the square to cover the filling, next fold over the top edge and lastly fold in the two remaining sides, one over the other so that the filling is now enveloped between the dough sheet.

Then, using a hot, heavy bottomed pan heat a little oil and fry the filled dough for a few minutes on each side until golden brown.

These can be eaten hot or cold.

Submitted by Umm Amine

Sweet recipes

Lamona (Algerian Brioche)

Ingredients

124ml warm milk

100ml warm water

1 egg, beaten

60g butter or margarine, melted

Zest of 1 lemon

70g sugar

425g strong plain flour

2 teaspoons easy blend yeast

12 chunks of dark chocolate

Method

I have a bread-maker so I put the ingredients above into the bread-machine in the order listed and use the pizza or dough setting. This setting will mix, kneed and rise the dough but will stop before baking.

Alternatively, mix the dry ingredients together, combine the wet ingredients and then gradually kneed the wet ingredients into the dry and kneed until you have a smooth, flexible dough and leave to rise in a warm place for 1 hour.

Once the cycle has ended, knock back the dough and cut into 12 pieces.

Put a chunk of dark chocolate in the centre of each piece of dough and shape into buns.

Place on a lightly floured baking tray and glaze with beaten egg and half a teaspoonful of sugar.

Leave to prove for another 30-60 mins and then bake at 400F for 15 mins or until they sound hollow when tapped.

Submitted by Umm Ibrahim

Kesra

A flat bread made from a mixture of semolina and flour.

Ingredients

250g plain flour

250g fine semolina

½ tsp salt

1 tbs baking powder

10 tbs olive oil

43 tbs warm water.

Method

Put all the dry ingredients in a large bowl and mix together. Make a well in the centre and add the oil. Mix together so that the oil is distributed evenly through the mixture. Add the water and mix together with your hands. The dough should be neither dry nor sticky add a little more water or semolina as necessary.

Tip out of the bowl and knead for approximately 10 minutes until the dough is smooth and elastic. Leave to rest for a further 10 minutes.

Roll the dough out (or shape with your hands) so that it forms a large circle approximately the size of a dinner plate. Prick all over the top and sides with a fork so that the steam can be released. Place the dough into a large, dry frying pan or crepe pan.

Dry fry each side on a medium heat for about 5-7 minutes until the bread is golden coloured.

Slice and serve. This bread is particularly nice with soup.

Submitted by Umm Hisham

Beghrir Express

Beghrir is a round pan cooked delight, very similar to the English Pikelet.

Ingredients

250g -1 cup fine or ultra fine semolina
120g - 1/2 cup all purpose flour
1/2 TBS instant yeast
1 package (10g - 2tsp) baking powder
pinch of baking soda

few capfuls of orange blossom water (or to taste)
generous 1 tsp vanilla
250mL-1 cup milk
250mL-1 cup warm water
pinch of salt
1-2 TBS sugar (optional)

(makes about 12)

Method

Add the liquids into a blender, then all the dry ingredients. Optionally use a stick blender.

Blend for a few minutes until the batter is homogenous.

Set the batter aside for about 15 minutes to proof.

After the 15 minutes, you should see little bubbles forming from the help of the yeast. This is when you know the batter is ready to use. If there are no bubbles, then your yeast may be old.

Turn on your fire and place your pan on the fire.

Ladle in the batter into the cold ungreased pan. I use a small ladle that is about 1/4 cup.

After a few seconds you will see the holes appear. And is cook in under a minute.

Now remove from the pan and place on a clean kitchen towel or parchment. Do not stack them - they will stick!

Repeat until you have used all the batter.

Once you have cooked off all the Beghrir, you can pour a mixture of honey and butter (equal parts) over the Beghrir.

Allow to soak in before serving.

Submitted by Henrietta Takács El-Ghoul

ORANGE CAKE

360G Self raising flour

180g sugar

120ml oil

3 eggs

5tbs water

2 Oranges –zest and juice

2 tsp vanilla sugar

1tbs baking powder

For the syrup

1 orange –zest and juice

1 tbs orange blossom water (Mazhar)

3 tbs sugar

10 tbs water

Method

Preheat oven to gas mark 5

In a large bowl mix together the eggs, oil and water plus the zest and juice of 2 oranges.

Add to the mix the flour, sugar, baking powder and vanilla sugar.

Stir thoroughly.

Pour the mixture into a greased tin. I like to use a 2lb loaf tin but, an 8" circular one would work just as well and is more traditional.

Bake for approximately 40 minutes or until golden and firm to touch.

Whilst the cake is baking prepare the syrup. Simply add the zest and juice of one orange, the water, sugar and orange blossom water in a pan and simmer for 10 minutes until a light, tangy syrup has formed.

Take the cake from the oven, remove from the tin and place on a cooling rack. With a skewer prick small holes all over the top of the cake. Pour the syrup all over. Leave to cool.

Submitted by Emma Waller

Makrout with Dates and Honey

Ingredients

350g fine or medium semolina

35g flour

1/8 teaspoon salt

160g melted butter or vegetable oil

160ml orange flower water

300g dates

1 tablespoon melted butter

1 tablespoon orange flower water

1/2 teaspoon cinnamon, or more to taste

vegetable oil, for frying

340g honey

1 tablespoon orange flower water

Method

Oil the semolina. Blend the semolina, flour and salt. Add the melted butter (or oil) and use your hands to toss and massage the mixture for several minutes to ensure that each grain of semolina is individually coated with the butter. If time allows, cover and set aside for an hour or longer before proceeding.

Make the dough. Again using your hands, gradually work the orange flower water into the semolina mixture. Don't knead, but do rake the semolina and mix/squeeze with your fingers to incorporate the liquid until a moist ball of dough forms and holds shape. (If necessary, you can add a little more water, a few teaspoons at a time, to achieve this.) Cover, and set the dough aside to rest for at least an hour while you make the date paste in the next step.

Make the date paste. Remove the pits from the dates, and place the dates in a steamer basket or metal colander which has been set over a pot of simmering water. Steam the dates, uncovered, for 20 to 30 minutes. Transfer the dates to a food processor, add the butter, orange flower water and cinnamon, and process until a smooth paste forms. Set the paste aside to cool.

Shape the cookies. When the date paste has cooled and firmed a bit, wet or oil your hands. Divide the paste into four portions, and shape each portion into a thin log about the same diameter of your finger.

Divide the dough into four portions. Take one, and gently shape it into a log the same length as a log of date paste. Make a deep indentation that runs the length of the dough and insert the date filling. Gently pinch the dough around the filling to enclose it (pinch off and discard any excess dough on the ends), then roll the dough back and forth a few times on your work surface to seal.

Heat the oil, fry the makrout lightly. Drain and dip into the honey.

Submitted by Riana Nel

Basbousa

Deliciously sweet diamond shaped cakes reminiscent of Syrup pudding, especially when eaten warm.

180g Butter

150g Sugar

10fl oz Buttermilk

240g Course Semolina

1 ½ tsp Vanilla essence

1 tbs Baking powder

1tbs Baking soda

<u>For the Syrup</u>

200g Sugar

Juice of 1 lemon

8fl oz water

Method

Pre-heat the oven at gas mark 4

Melt the butter in the pan and allow to cool a little.

In a large bowl mix together the Sugar and buttermilk. Add to this the semolina, vanilla essence, baking powder and baking soda. Mix thoroughly. Add the melted butter to the mixture and stir in.

Grease and line a tin. Pour the mixture in and let sit for approximately 20 minutes.

Place in the oven and bake for 30 minutes or until firm and lightly golden.

Whilst the Basbousa is baking prepare the syrup by putting the sugar, lemon juice, water and orange flower water (if using) into a saucepan. Simmer over a medium heat until a light syrup has formed.

The syrup should be poured over whilst the cake is still warm. Allow to cool and slice into pieces, traditionally they are diamond shaped but squares work equally well.

Submitted by Umm Amina

Mchakek

These are delightful little sweets which taste similar to marzipan. These can be prepared well in advance as they 'keep' for ages!

Ingredients

200g ground Almonds

100g Sugar

½ tsp Vanilla sugar

2 egg whites

6 tbs icing sugar

12 nuts of choice

Few drops of food colouring.

(makes 12)

Method

Pre –heat the oven to gas mark 5.

Mix the ground almonds, vanilla and sugar together in a large bowl. Add the food colouring and gradually add the egg whites until the mixture holds together (you may not need to use all of the egg whites).

Make into walnut sized balls and place individually into paper cases, top each with a nut.

Place on a baking tray and bake for approximately 15 minutes, just until the cakes set but still remain pale.

Cool on a wire rack, store in an airtight container or enjoy straight away!

Submitted by Emma Waller

Mhalbi (Algerian Rice Pudding)

Ingredients

190g ground rice

1 litre milk

200g sugar

3 drops rose water

Cinnamon, ground

Method

Pour the milk into a saucepan and put over a medium heat. Add the ground rice and sugar and stir until it thickens. Add the rose water and take the pan off the heat. Serve in ramekins and decorate with cinnamon.

Submitted Kaouter Hachemi

M'halbi (Algerian rice pudding) #2
serves 6
Ingredients

50g of rice powder
3 tablespoons cornstarch
1 litre of milk
pinch of cinnamon
1 vanilla sugar
3 tablespoon of sugar (or honey)
2 tablespoons orange flower water
50 g ground almonds
Decorations: pistachios, almonds, sultana, dates, cinnamon, etc

Method

Pour the milk into a heavy bottom pot.
Place the corn starch in a cup; add a little water to dissolve it.
Now add the remaining ingredients to the pot.
Bring the milk to boil.
Constantly stir until it is thick.

Pour into cups/bowls.

Decorate as desired then let sit for 30m before eating.

Submitted by Henrietta Takács El-Ghoul

Griweche

This recipe requires some patience, but the result is worth it both in terms of taste and looks. It uses two common ingredients in Algerian cakes: rose water and sesame seeds and is always found in Algerian households on special occasions, particularly Eid Al Fitr.

Ingredients

4 bowls flour

1 bowl butter

Pinch salt

1 egg

3 drops rose water or vanilla extract

Oil for deep frying

Honey or syrup

Sesame seeds, toasted

Method

Rub the butter into the flour and salt. Add the egg and rose water or vanilla and mix until it forms a smooth dough. Form into almond-sized balls. Roll each ball into a sausage (about 5 mm in diameter), then twist to form a pretzel-like shape. Deep fry until golden and place on kitchen towel to soak up any extra oil. While still hot, dip the Griweche in the honey until covered then sprinkle generously with sesame seeds. Cool and serve with mint tea.

Submitted Kaouter Hachemi

Filled sables

Soft buttery biscuits traditionally filled with jam although chocolate spread and lemon curd can also make nice alternatives.

Ingredients

200g butter

100g sugar

300g plain flour

1 tsp baking powder

1 egg

5g vanilla sugar

3 heaped tbs jam

3 tbs icing sugar

1tsp water

(makes approximately 20 biscuits)

Method

Preheat the oven to gas mark 5

In a bowl cream the sugar, butter, vanilla sugar and egg together.

Sift the flour and baking powder into the bowl and mix thoroughly until a dough forms.

The dough should be soft but still manageable. If the dough feels too soft add a dash more flour. If necessary chill in the fridge for ten minutes so that it can firm up a little.

Roll out the dough so that it is approximately 1cm thick. Using a cutter or upturned glass cut out circles of the dough. Place half of the cut out circles onto a lined baking tray.

Using a smaller cutter or the lid of a bottle cut out the centres of the remaining half and then place these onto the baking tray too.

Bake in the oven for approximately 8-10 minutes. The biscuits should are ready to take out when they are set but still pale. They should not be golden in colour.

Place on a wire rack to cool.

Place 3 heaped tablespoons of jam and 1 teaspoon of water to a small saucepan, allow it to boil over a low heat.

While the jam is boiling take the biscuit rounds with holes in the middle and dust the tops with icing sugar and set aside. These will be the tops.

Place a blob of jam in the centre of the remaining biscuits and add a top to each. Allow the jam to cool slightly and then enjoy!

These biscuits will 'keep' for a week if kept in an airtight container.

Submitted by Emma Waller

Algerian Shortbread

This is slightly different from Scottish shortbread as eggs are used in addition to butter. But like its Scottish counterpart, it is a delicious, chunky biscuit that is perfect with tea or coffee.

This recipe includes chopped pistachio nuts but any nuts could be used and indeed raisins or chocolate chips could be tasty alternatives.

Ingredients

3 eggs

160g sugar

160g butter

¼ tsp salt

225g plain flour

1 tsp baking powder

50g roughly chopped pistachio nuts

(Makes approximately 24 biscuits depending on cutter size)

Method

In a bowl mix the eggs and sugar together.

Sieve in the flour, salt and baking powder, Mix together thoroughly.

Stir in the chopped nuts

Rub in the butter until a soft dough forms, if the mixture seems a little dry add some cold water a teaspoon at a time until it all comes together.

Wrap in cling film and chill for 20 minutes

Roll out the dough and cut out rounds approximately 1cm thick using a biscuit cutter or up turned glass.

Place on a lined baking tray and bake at gas mark 5 for approximately 15 minutes. The biscuits are done when the dough has set but not coloured.

Leave to cool on a wire rack.

Submitted by Emma Waller

Kalb el louz

This is a very moist cake made from almonds and semolina. Traditionally it is eaten during Ramadan but it can of course, be enjoyed all year round.

Ingredients

500g course semolina

225g granulated sugar

100g ground almonds

125ml water

5 tbs orange blossom water

140g butter

1 tsp vanilla extract

For the syrup

500ml water

150g granulated sugar

8 tbs orange blossom water

3 tbs honey

Method

Melt the butter and allow it to cool.

Pre heat the oven to 180 degrees

In a large bowl mix together the semolina, almonds and granulated sugar.

Add to this the melted butter and mix thoroughly.

Add the vanilla

In a jug mix the water and orange blossom water together. Gradually pour the liquid into the bowl and mix with the other ingredients.

Press the dough into a baking tray or dish, whichever you prefer. The dough should be approximately 3cm in height.

Score into squares and top each section with an almond half if using.

Bake in the oven for approximately 45 minutes or until the surface is golden brown.

While the cake is baking prepare the syrup by placing the water, honey, sugar and orange blossom water in a pan, boil and then simmer until light syrup has formed.

Once the cake is done pour the syrup over the top, this will have to be done gradually to allow the liquid to be absorbed. It may seem like a lot of syrup but do use it all, this cake is supposed to be very moist and if you don't use it all the bottom of the cake will be dry.

Allow to cool and then slice into portions.

Submitted by Umm Meryam

Halkouma

Delicately flavoured jelly sweets.

Ingredients

50g cornflower

100g granulated sugar

200ml water

4tbs orange blossom water or rose water

Few drops of food colouring

Method

Put all of the ingredients into a non-stick pot and cook over a low heat.

Allow to simmer for approximately 20 minutes stirring periodically.

Gradually the mixture will begin thickening, lumps will appear but that isn't a problem so do not worry. Once all the ingredients have come together as a solid form in the middle of the pot tip it out and press into a dish or baking tray.

Allow to cool and set for several hours, overnight if possible. Do not refrigerate just leave it out in a cool place.

Once set slice into chunks and dust with icing sugar or if preferred roll in granulated sugar.

Store in a cool place.

Makes approximately 15 sweets

Submitted by Yasmina Tanzir

Mchewek

Little lemon and almond flavoured cakes topped off with a glace cherry.

Ingredients

200g ground almonds

100g granulated sugar

Grated zest of 2 lemons

2 small eggs

100g flaked almonds

Glace cherries to decorate

Method

Preheat the oven to gas mark 5

Add the ground almonds, sugar and lemon zest to a bowl and mix together.

Gradually add the eggs until the mixture comes together, you may not need to use all of it.

Shape into walnut sized balls and roll in the flaked almonds. Flatten slightly and top with half a glace cherry.

Bake for approximately 15 minutes. The cakes are done when they are set and just lightly coloured. Cool on a wire rack.

Submitted by Emma Waller

Makrout el louz

These are my all time favourite! Delicious diamond shaped cakes made from almonds and tangy limes finished off with several dustings of icing sugar.

Ingredients

(Makes 10)

200g ground almonds

100g granulated sugar

Grated zest of 2 limes

2 small eggs

300g icing sugar

For the syrup

100g Granulated sugar

3 tbs. Orange flower water

5 fl. Oz.Water

Method

Preheat the oven to gas mark 5.

Put the sugar and ground almonds in a bowl, mix together.

Add the lime zest and stir through.

Gradually add the eggs, the mixture should just hold together so all of the eggs may not be necessary.

Form the mixture into a cylinder shape approximately 25" long. Flatten the top so that it becomes rectangular. Slice into diamonds of equal size.

Place the diamond shapes onto a lined baking tray and bake for approximately 15 minutes. The cakes should be just set and still pale when they are done.

Whilst the cakes are baking make the syrup by boiling the water, sugar and orange flower water together in a pan for 5 minutes or until a light syrup has formed.

Once the cakes are baked, while still warm dip them into the syrup and then into the icing sugar. The whole cake should be covered with icing sugar. Leave to dry on a wire rack.

Once dry dust the cakes with a further layer of icing sugar.

Place into paper cases and serve.

Submitted by Emma Waller

Nadia's cakes

These do have an official name but, in my house they are always referred to as 'Nadia's cakes' in reference to my sister in Law Nadia who introduced them to me and who never fails to make me a huge batch whenever I visit Algeria.

Ingredients

100g bimo biscuits / rich tea biscuits

200g halva

60g butter

2 tbs orange blossom water

100g desiccated coconut

150g milk chocolate

Method

Crush the biscuits and place in a bowl.

Crumble the halva into the bowl and mix thoroughly with the crushed biscuit.

Add the orange blossom water and the butter to the bowl and mix. The ingredients should just come together, if it's a little difficult just keep pressing and mixing, do not add more butter.

Form into balls a little smaller in size than a walnut. Chill in the fridge for 30 minutes.

Melt the chocolate and thinly coat the balls in it, roll in the coconut and allow to set.

These keep well if stored in an air tight container.

Submitted by Emma Waller

H'rissa

A no-bake sweet that is very quick and easy to make. Traditionally almonds are used but these could be replaced with other types of nuts. I personally have had lots of success using coconut as an alternative.

Ingredients

1 egg white

100g ground almonds

100g sugar

Food colouring of choice

1 tsp flavouring (optional)

Extra sugar for dusting

Silver balls or nut pieces (optional)

Method

Put the sugar and ground almonds in a bowl and stir until thoroughly mixed together.

Add the food colouring and flavouring if using, stir in.

Gradually add the egg white until the mixture comes together, you may not need to use all of it.

The mixture should be a little sticky but still very manageable.

Roll into small walnut sized balls.

Lightly press down on the centre of the ball so it is slightly flattened. Then with a teaspoon or bottle top make diagonal indentations around the edges.

Roll the sweet in the sugar and top with silver balls if using.

Store in an air tight container.

Submitted by Umm Meryam